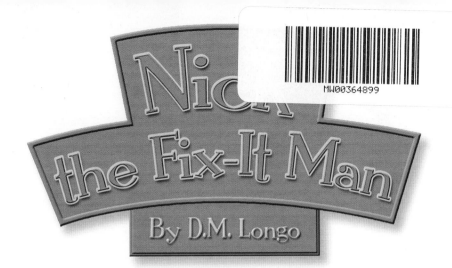

By D.M. Longo

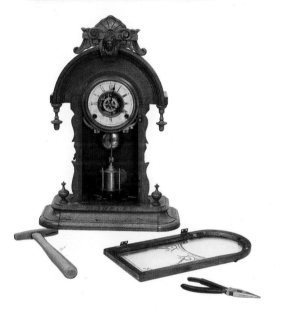

Target Skill Sequence

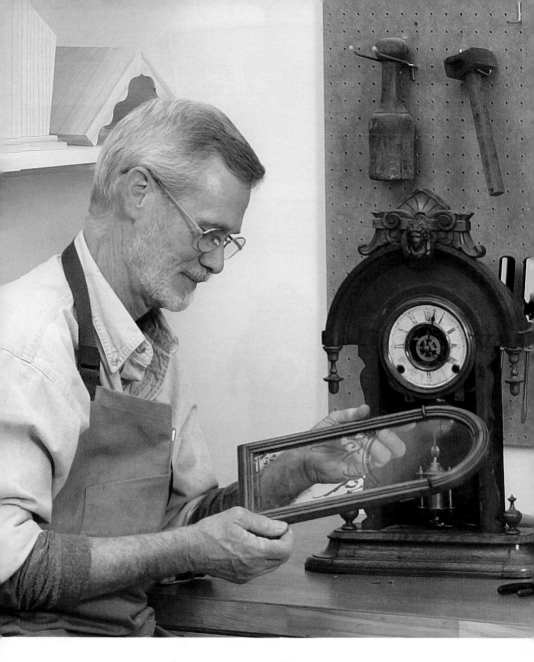

Nick is a fix-it man!

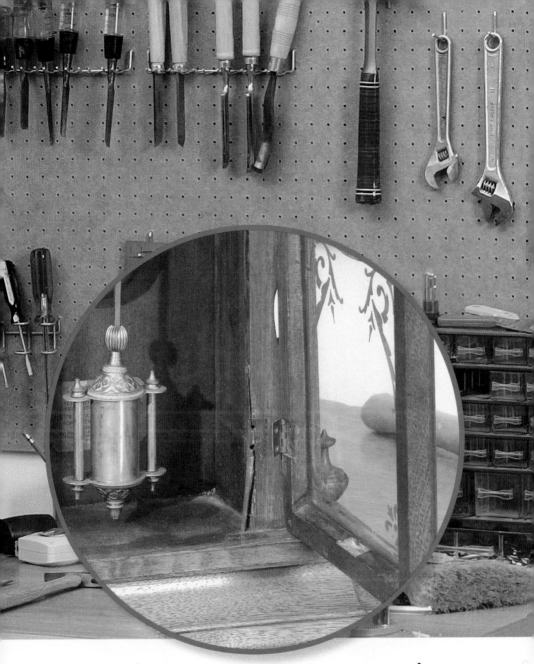

Nick can see a crack
in the clock.

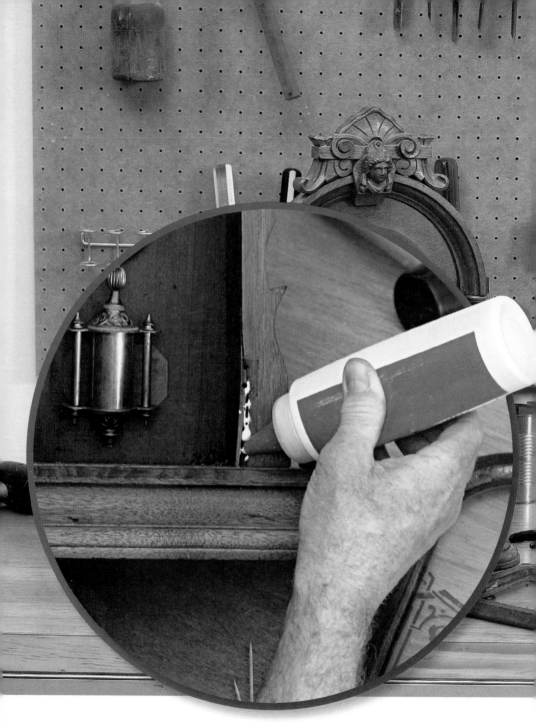

Nick can fix the little crack.

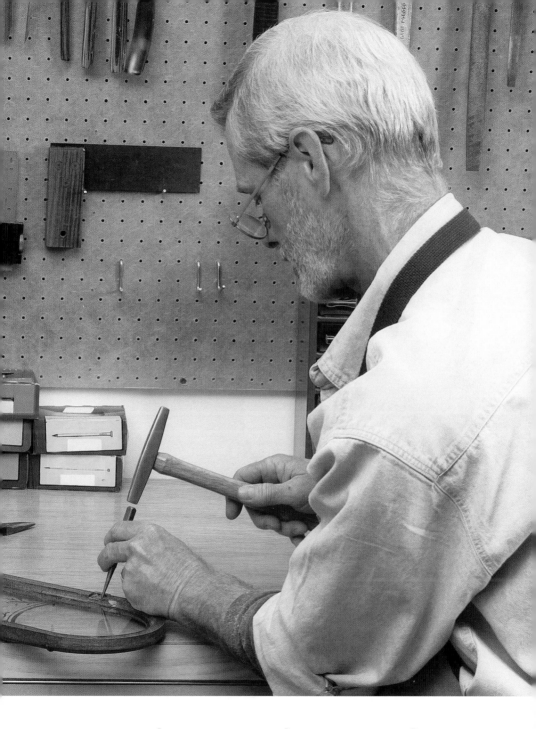

Smack, smack, smack!

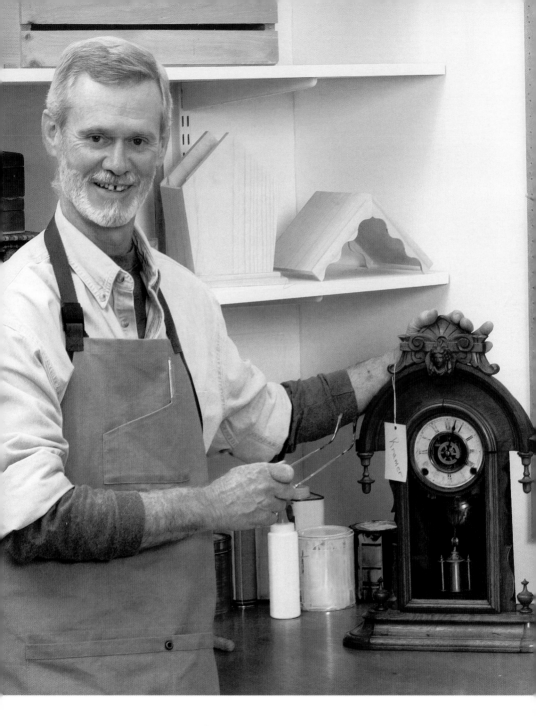

Nick fixed the clock!

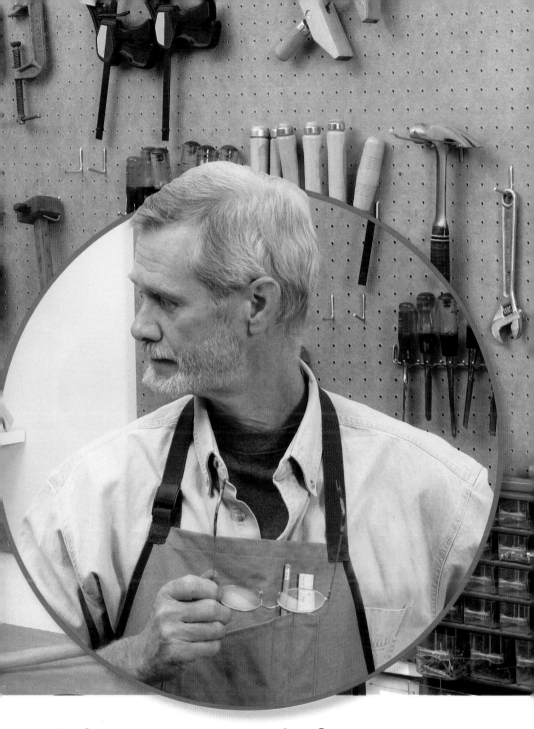

What can Nick fix now?

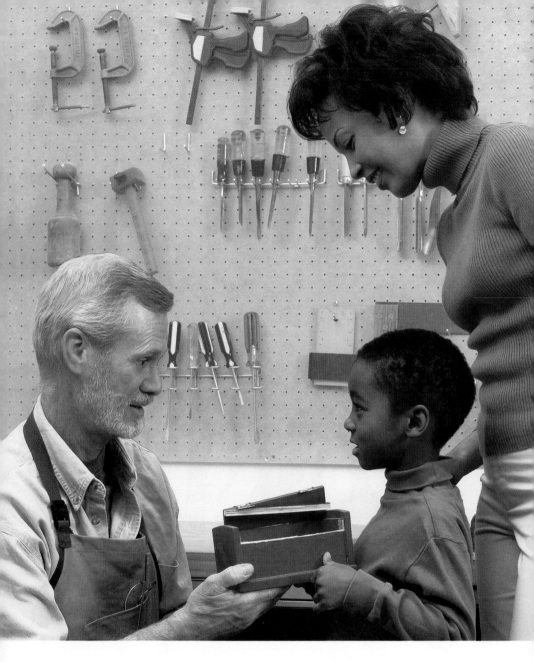

Max has a little box
for Nick to fix.